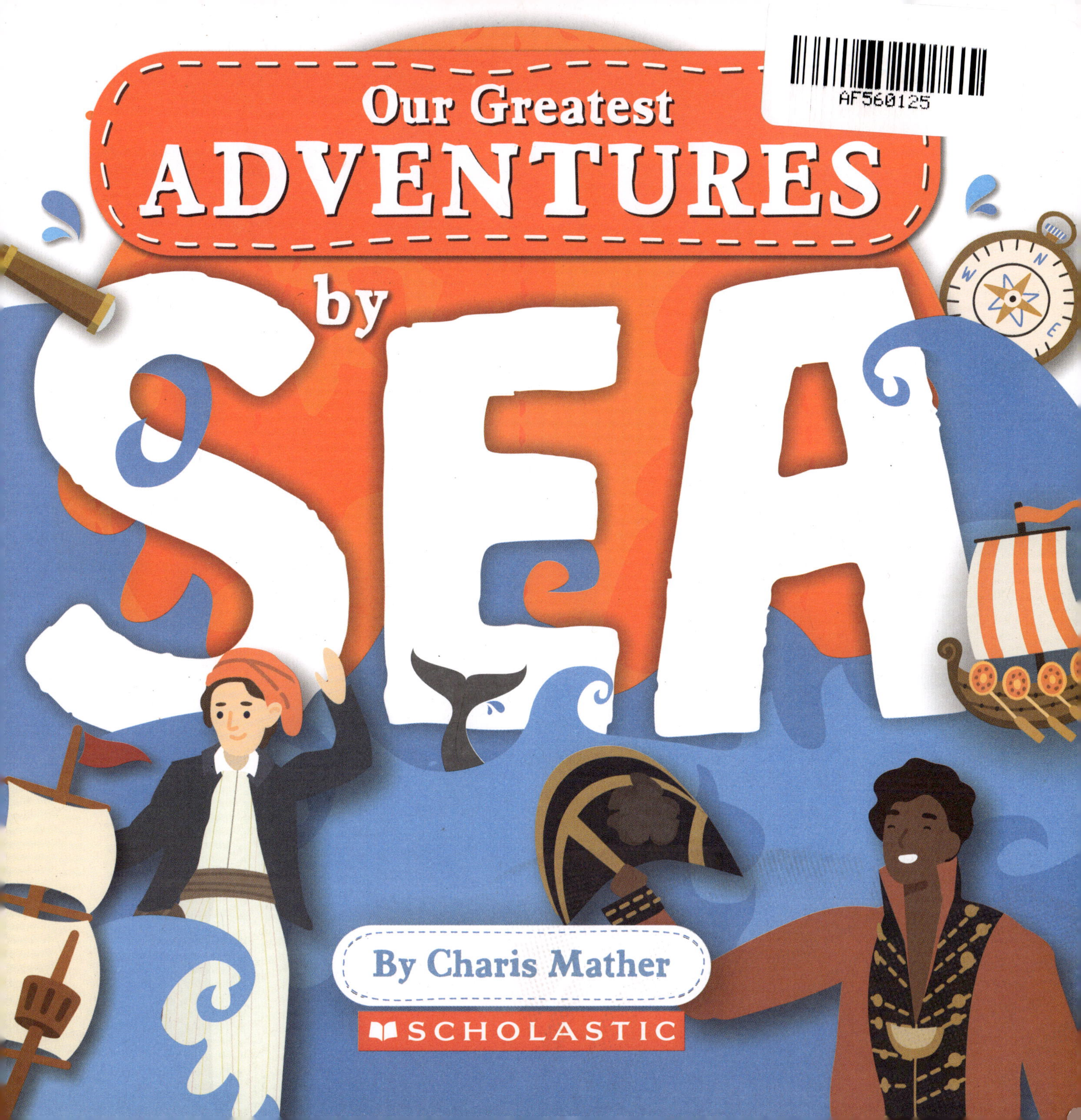
Our Greatest
ADVENTURES
by
SEA
By Charis Mather
SCHOLASTIC
W
N
E

King's Lynn, Norfolk
PE30 4LS, UK

A catalogue record for this book is available from the British Library.

Published and Distributed in India by Scholastic India Pvt. Ltd.

This Reprint Edition: Dec. 2024

ISBN: 978-93-5954-064-1

Written by: Charis Mather

Edited by: William Anthony

Designed by: Amy Li

Printed in India at

MicroPrints India, New Delhi

CONTENTS

Words that look like <u>this</u> can be found in the glossary on page 24.

OUR GREATEST ADVENTURES BY SEA

Have you ever been on a boat? You have probably spent more time on land than in a boat, but most of the world is covered by water. We have still not explored it all.

Lots of people in history have travelled on the seas. Some have even gone under the water to explore. We can learn a lot from the people who have been on such amazing adventures.

LEIF ERIKSON

Born: Around 970 Died: Around 1020

Leif Erikson was a Viking. He was the son of Erik the Red, who was famous for discovering the country Greenland. Erikson also became famous when he took a ship to an unexplored land.

Leif Erikson was from Iceland.

A Viking called Bjarni Herjólfsson told Erikson about this new land across the sea. Erikson set sail for what is now called North America. When he arrived, he named the place Vinland.

ZHENG HE

Born: 1371
Died: Around 1433

Zheng He was a Chinese man who was put in charge of the emperor's huge treasure ships. Zheng He went on seven journeys on the ocean so that people would see the emperor's power.

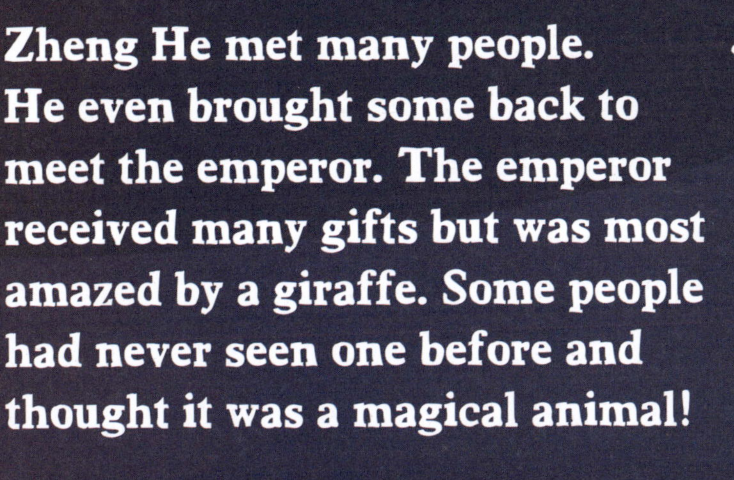

Zheng He met many people. He even brought some back to meet the emperor. The emperor received many gifts but was most amazed by a giraffe. Some people had never seen one before and thought it was a magical animal!

Be Inspired!

TRY TO MEET PEOPLE WHO LIVE DIFFERENTLY TO YOU.

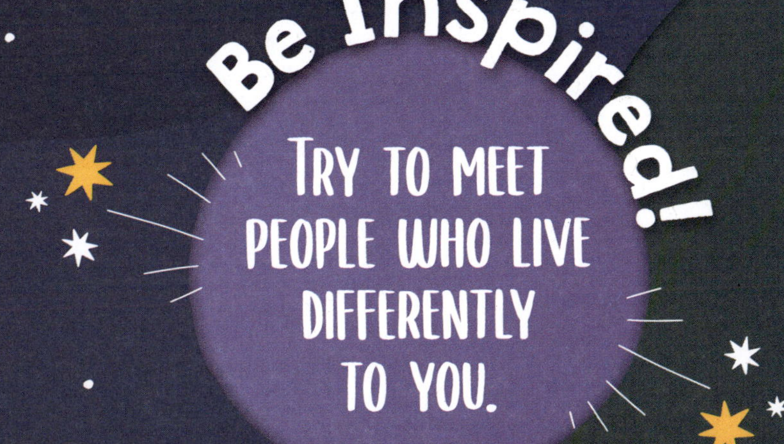

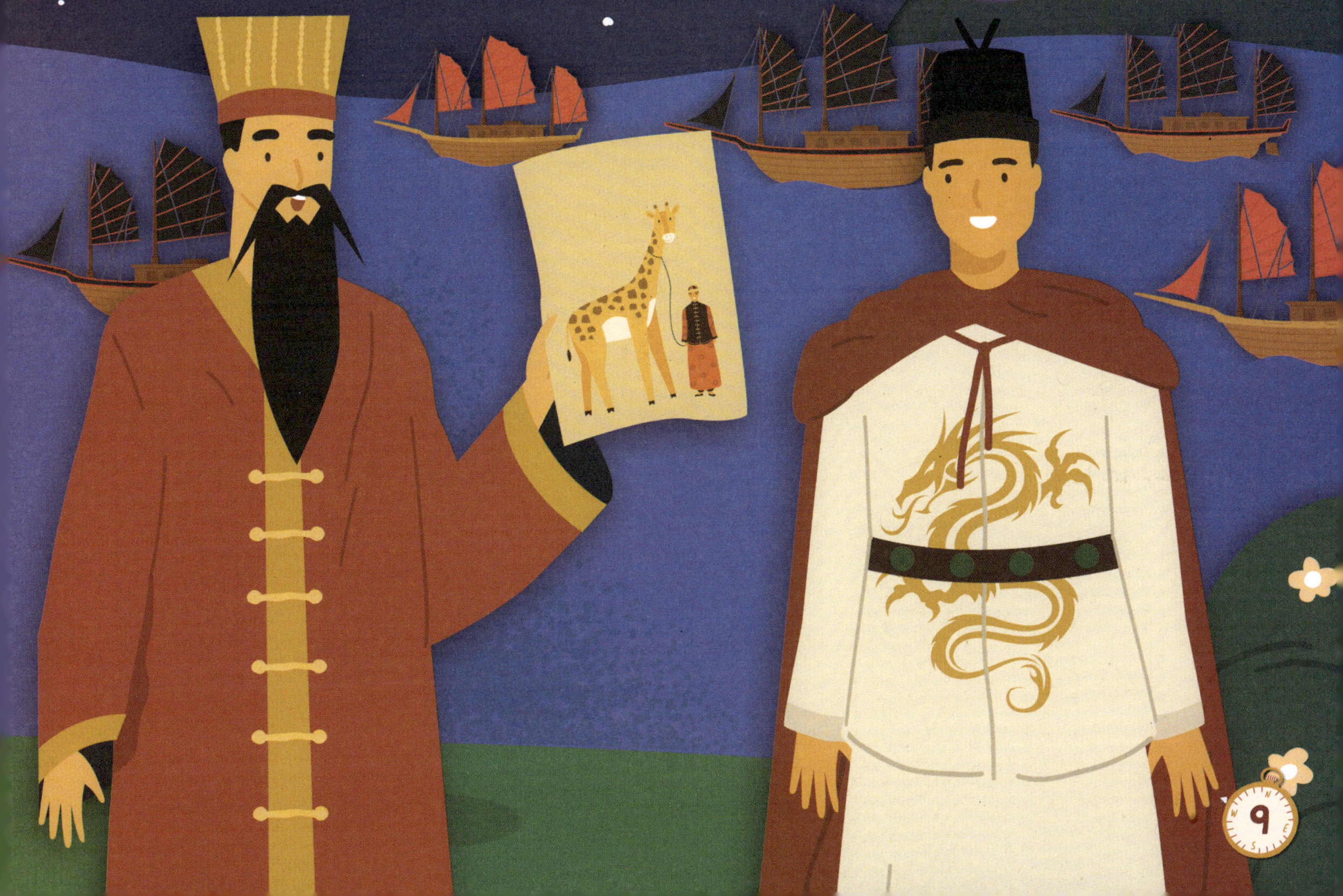

FERDINAND MAGELLAN

Born: 1480
Died: 1521

When Ferdinand Magellan was born, no one had ever travelled the whole way around the world. Magellan wanted to try. He took some ships on a new route that no one knew would work.

Ferdinand Magellan was from Portugal.

Magellan's ships crossed the huge Pacific Ocean. The people ran out of food but found land after 99 days. Magellan died soon after, but the navigator, Elcano, took the last ship back to finish the journey.

JEANNE BARET

Born: 1740
Died: 1807

Jeanne Baret was the first woman to sail around the world. Baret's partner, Philibert Commerson, had joined a trip to go around the world. Baret wanted to go with him, but women were not allowed.

Baret wore a disguise to look like a man so she could sail with Commerson. On their journey, Baret and Commerson found and studied plants. Now, there is a flower named after her.

Be Inspired!

LEARN TO THINK OF CREATIVE ANSWERS TO PROBLEMS.

BUNGAREE

Born: 1775
Died: 1830

Bungaree was the first Aboriginal Australian to sail all the way around Australia. He travelled with Captain Matthew Flinders. Bungaree would often joke around and try to make people laugh.

On their journey, they would sometimes see Aboriginal people. Bungaree left the ship to meet them. If he did not speak their language, he used hand signs to show that he was peaceful.

FABIAN GOTTLIEB VON BELLINGSHAUSEN

Born: 1778
Died: 1852

Fabian Gottlieb von Bellingshausen was a Russian captain who went on a trip to Antarctica. He was the first person to see the main continent. Others had tried but found the icy waters too dangerous.

Von Bellingshausen's journey took over two years. He met some Aboriginal people on the way and bought food from them. Even though there were bad storms, von Bellingshausen was able to sail around Antarctica.

Be Inspired!

DO NOT GIVE UP, EVEN IF SOMETHING LOOKS IMPOSSIBLE.

WILLIAM BEEBE

Born: 1877
Died: 1962

People long ago did not know much about deep-sea creatures. William Beebe was an American scientist who studied life under the ocean. He and Otis Barton invented something called a bathysphere to help them.

The bathysphere was a metal ball that took Beebe and Barton into the ocean. Even though it was dangerous, they were excited to see new animals through the windows. Beebe and Barton set a record for the deepest dive.

DR SYLVIA EARLE

Born: 1935

Dr Sylvia Earle is an explorer and oceanographer. An oceanographer is a scientist who learns about the oceans and the life in them. Earle has spent thousands of hours diving under the water.

Earle once went on a dive and walked around the ocean floor. She went in a special deep-water suit. Earle's dive was a record, since no one had done that below 380 metres before.

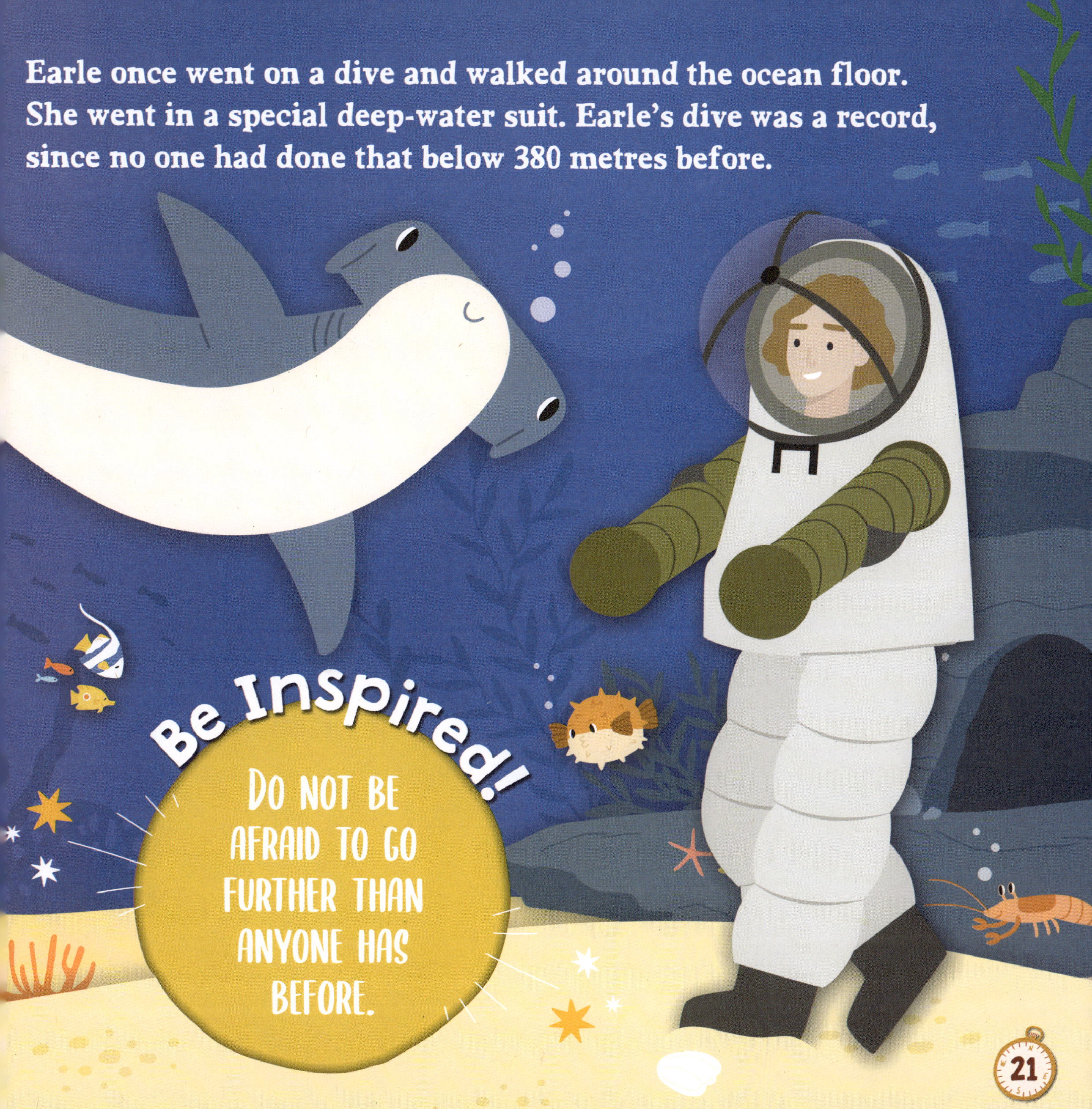

YOUR GREATEST ADVENTURE BY SEA

People have been adventuring by sea for hundreds of years. Some have been on ships to find new places. Some have been underwater to learn about our world.

There are still many ocean adventures to go on. It is time for you to plan your own!

Use a finger to plan your own adventure by sea on this map.

Who will you travel with?

Where will you go? Point to it on the map.

Will you travel in a boat or dive under the water?

GLOSSARY

Aboriginal	the first people to ever live in a place
continent	a large area of land, such as Antarctica, Africa or Europe, that is often made up of many countries
disguise	an outfit that hides what someone really looks like
emperor	a person who rules over lots of land and people
explored	travelled to and found out about new places
navigator	a person who is in charge of planning and controlling where a ship travels
Pacific Ocean	the large area of water between North America, South America, Oceania and Asia
record	the best or farthest something has been done
route	a way to get from one place to another
scientist	a person who learns and knows a lot about science
studied	learned about something

INDEX

Photo Credits. Images are courtesy of Shutterstock.com. With thanks to GettyImages, ThinkstockPhoto and iStockphoto. Throughout – GoodStudio, mhatzapa. Cover – Kate Demanovska, Kate Garyuk, TDubov. 6–7 – Ivan Marc, Sabelskaya. 8–9 – enciktat, NotionPic, vectornes. 10–11 – Naci Yavuz, VectorShow, Meilun. 12–13 – Sudowoodo, Cristoforo Dall'Acqua (WikiCommons). 14–15 – Macrovector, Augustus EARLE (WikiCommons). 16–17 – Olga Popova, Meilun. 18–19 – Wildlife Conservation Society (WikiCommons), funkyplayer, Ruslan__Grebeshkov. 20–21 – Bonnie L. Campbell (WikiCommons). 22–23 – Viacheslav Lopatin.